BLUR

ALSO BY DOUG RAMSPECK:

Book of Years
Under Black Leaves
Distant Fires
The Owl That Carries Us Away
Black Flowers
Original Bodies
Mechanical Fireflies
Possum Nocturne
Where We Come From
Black Tupelo Country

BLUR

Doug Ramspeck

THE WORD WORKS
WASHINGTON, D.C.

THE WORD WORKS
P.O. Box 42164
Washington, D.C. 20015
editor@wordworksbooks.org

Cover design: Susan Pearce
Cover art: Photograph by Johannes Plenio
Author photograph: Beth Sutton-Ramspeck

ISBN 978-1-944585-60-0
LCCN 2022931865

Acknowledgments

Grateful acknowledgment is made to the editors of the following publications where the poems in this collection were originally published.

American Literary Review: "the art of divination," "dream of the ten rivers," "Grass Prayers," and "renunciation."

Asheville Poetry Review: "Music of the Orchard."

Beloit Poetry Journal: "the brothers fall in love," "father gets drunk with the moon," and "Winter Trance."

Boulevard: "family anthem" and "Snow Synopsis."

The Carolina Quarterly: "Prayer Book."

Cimarron Review: "Earthly Displays," "History," and "Old Mud."

The Cincinnati Review: "Anthem (Snow)," "History of the Wheel," and "The Marriage We Carried in Our Pockets."

Colorado Review: "The Old Worlds" and "spume."

Cortland Review: "Anthem," "Dialogue and Asymmetry," "Divining the Mountain," and "white sky."

Crazyhorse: "Grass Alchemy" and "ontological snow."

December Magazine: "blind the years" and "drowned boy."

Faultline: "In the Kingdom."

FIELD: "Chicago."

Gulf Coast: "Ghost Fire."

Hotel Amerika: "Tethered" and "Wind Metaphysics."

Iron Horse Literary Review: "fly-over states of mind" and "Winter Fingerprints."

The Laurel Review: "sister rides her stick horse toward eternity," "snow prophecy," "the moon opens and closes its gates," and "yellowjacket dreams."

Literary Imagination: "Mud Words."

Massachusetts Review: "Blur" and "moon sonnet."

Mid-American Review: "City by the Sea."

Missouri Review: "Winter Country."

Natural Bridge: "Five Omens in Nine Days."

North American Review: "this town is roadkill fed on by crows."

Pleiades: "father beats his sons beneath an unmoored moon."

The Shore: "the midwest hangs itself while listening to the bobolinks,"
    "signs," "the old men climb a flight of stairs to go to bed,"
    "the brothers try to drown each other at guthrie quarry."
Tampa Review: "Primitive Prayers."
TriQuarterly: "black cloth of sky" and "feral trains."
Tupelo Quarterly: "the brothers' one true home is inside their bodies,"
    "the geography where the boys live includes an unlatched
    gate," and "there is inside the boys a trajectory."

Contents

iii.

iv.

for Beth and Lee

Blur

So this is how we grew afraid.
The moon wore its bright hat.

The sun was a great wheel
of fire. Children played jump rope

in the streets, and everywhere
was the autobiographical,

the belief in the singular life
we knew as ours, the skin

pierced by hours then years.
At night when we lay close,

we whispered in the language
of relinquishment, prayed to all

the things we coveted. If this
was the dream, we could not

disavow it. If this was the torch,
we could not dare to light it.

Snow Synopsis

I was born in a snowstorm.
And so the white scarf went out across the land.

And the hours were a physiognomy I could not read.
And then I was five and lived in a meadow

beneath a dome of clouds that lived
in a meadow of sky. My thoughts, each day,

were simple as piano wire, and I dreamed
that I'd emerged into the world

from an opening in a hollow log,
that all the years were wood salt, that gravity

was the voice of my heart beating faster.
At twelve I fell in love with the way prayers

existed separate from the body, were the sounds of owls
in the woods, were everywhere a dark voyage

that brought me back where I'd begun.
But still a breath was an omen that floated in winter,

and hands were occultations, and the augury
of snow kept reaching down and down

to claim the land. I imagined snow
was an absence, was the white angel of the self,

the contour of a mind. But soon
I was seventeen and stepped into a field

and could not breathe. The air was so cold
it was holy, and the black hair of night

drooped down across the shoulders
of every hour. A life is like that, I understood.

When I married in my twenties, the drifts
of snow piled high against the fence,

but still the snow became a kiss against my face
and lips, and still I wanted to crawl back into that log

and disappear, but somehow I was forty
then sixty and blessed with prayers that never left

the earth but still existed all around me, and the closed
doors of decades whispered close against my ear

in falling snow while the disassembling days
were slipping one into another.

spume

in summer rain-weather the neighbor boy drowned   & the river said
see how my cattails bend in the current

& the river said
i carry your dead in my arms

& the river was visible from the house   & the brown hurry said
i exist beneath the fat gods of the low-slung clouds

& sister stood at the window & thought
these clouds are an owl digging its talons into back flesh

& the brothers stood at the window & thought
dead boy   dead

& the dead boy who was no longer in the river said
the years are something listing in a dusty cellar jar

& mother walked down to the river & thought
if you squeeze a tomato in your fist it bleeds

& father walked down to the river & thought
i didn't know you had it in you

& father remembered dragging a catfish once from that river & thinking
you are dead but don't know it yet

& father remembered stomping on the head of the fish with a boot that said
mercy

& the river said
dusk light is clinging to my body

& the river said
here is my premonition

& the boys walked down to the river & said to the spume
sing your death song   river

& the river said
this is my trumpet and my measure

& the river said
this is my eyehole to the world

& the river said
i am a river   a river   a river

The poets trace the body
& use pretty metaphors
for their lack of knowledge
The priest went to sleep
and the thought of God.
The scientist must not speak
of the aphoric descriptions
of a poet's love of the
notel of soul, unfound
in the body. Will we
the praise that the
truest be ere suffering
for the anxieties of
great life or
eternity is the
cells of bodies

Pascal's wager.

There was only white swans
when my father prayed for sanity
In another world there was a black one
and no one prayed for a miracle.
The limits of empiricism the holy man
says is the limit of imagination.
An n of 1 shows the ignorance of a limited world
and the empiricist in me would agree.
A cultish colour, controlled by,
like a raging lunatic barking at the moon.
But after all this time and lack of evidence
the difficulty of explaining the statistics of murder
is the gambit not to increase the holy in every earthly finding
& one miracle serves as proof of existence.
God hiding undiscoverable among so much hope,
& search party of the world not be found in atoms,
the secular god particle or the sunday morning mantuhas
The stoicism of science that
would grant possibility in all this absence
Is like a believer despite the Joban world.

Winter Country

We imagine, now, that our long dead are like the smell of woodsmoke

in the distance. And always there are signs: the snow pale

as masks, the attendant wind carving drifts into sharp blades.

The dead must seem obliged to live on inside the coating of winter

ice on naked limbs, in the loop of a sleeping snake curled beneath

a back porch. In my dreams my father burrows into the rotting

log that decays in the primitive loam of the woods. I hear him tapping

with the woodpeckers, hear the torn cry of a coyote at dusk.

All sensation exists on the edge of sleep, this erasure when the eyes

fall shut, the snow you cannot see as it covers up the world.

fly-over states of mind

i have spent a lifetime   inside my thoughts

inside a wheelbarrow   i can't seem to push

out of its rut   of days   & if there is some

thought proximity   some thought approximate

in which each new idea is embalmed   in its own juices

& if its toxicology   is spittle & sweat

& rain   then why can't i roll the wheelbarrow

forward then back   to get it careening over

the high ledge   & why do i suspect   that what

i would find   on the other side   would be another rut

& another hill   with the slope

of its incline   shaped like longing

family anthem

sister believes her brothers are the brackish waters of the river   are the possum fa

of the moon   & she believes that dusk light congeals inside their throats

once she saw them set fire to the neighbor's cat   saw them dance around the flar

& she dreamed that night that their teeth crumbled in their mouths like stones

that the stars were kicked over & abandoned   & she believes that the years

have soot-black tongues   that her brothers have soot-black tongues   & the son

they sing spill bitter salt into the world   once she might have smothered ther

in their cribs   might have dropped them like anthems from windows   once sh

watched them swim beneath a canker-sore of sun & she thought *let the mud wat*

carry them away   carry them under   & she dreamed that night

that they were standing by her bed   were carefully dousing her with lighter flui

& they said *we anoint you*   & she said *stop*   & they said *we baptize you*

& she said *you are not my brothers*   & they said *hush hush*

Music of the Orchard

As a boy I would see them sometimes
carrying blankets through the orchard,

walking through our yard toward the river,
and I would imagine that the dusk light

was a hand touching the braille
of the treetops, the living grass.

And I was old enough to imagine
that the way bees swarmed around

fallen globes of fruit was the way
the lovers joined their bodies

along the bank. My father told me
once that mud was the only prayer

that mattered, that our lives
were made of it, and the lovers,

I imagined, dreamed that the black
hair of the sky was a kind of ladder,

that the moonlight was a ladder
too, and the dirt beneath

their moving bodies was a prophet.
Come winter, I knew, I would hear

the music of the wind whipping across
the snow amid the trees, wailing

through window jambs, but in summer
I watched the distant birds sewing

the needles of their wings into
the clouds, studied the wildflowers

growing along the river where the lovers
lay down in darkness, the words

they whispered close against an ear
like the sounds of water over stone.

dream of the ten rivers

the boys summon vultures like bedclothes   wear them
in their sleep   wear them to wade into the dark current of the night

& so their father unfolds his wings inside their dreams   & a wreckage
of darkness gathers with a heatless fire

until the brothers exist almost wholly
inside wariness   inside boy smells

& they acquiesce to the dreamed hand
lashing toward them   to the caress of fists   to the blood-taste in the mouth

& the story they tell is of wildfire   of ten rivers   the water spreading outward
like fingers on hands   rivers of numerology

or they tell the story of the blind prophet who sees only
that there is no way out   that the years are waxen ghosts

or they sit with their father at the kitchen table   sit with their father
on the porch   sit with their father in his truck

until sitting becomes a kind of prayer   until the silence of their voices
is a kind of prayer

& the vultures draw the pink entrails from the carcasses   conjure
perfect strings of them   strings to tie around fingers in remembrance

& the brothers want to swim with their father in the current   to be their father
in the current   & also to be the vultures with their shaved heads

& when it snows in winter the brothers will skate the ten rivers
with sharp blades   blades that draw blood from the ice

& their father will come to them in their dreams   will crack the surface
with heavy boots   will whisper comfort as he holds them
fast beneath

snow prophecy

mother imagines that the snowflakes falling
behind the house are her children

& the snow hardening into a carapace of skin
is a kind of long division   the years

existing in the backs of her teeth   in a throb
in her molars   in some raw patch of her tongue

or maybe her children are the sticky eggs
of stars embedded in the sky's mud

or the trees in the woods shed not only
their leaves but their bark   stripped to bare bone

& when she was younger she imagined that a body
growing inside another body might come to seem

like prophecy   & she imagined something holy
in the blood of giving birth   something sacrificial

but now she wonders if her sons & her daughter
are more like smoke or mist, not a plinth

but constructed out of visions and winter snows
& she suspects that the years are something

you might catch in an outstretched palm
& the filial devotion of the sky

makes of her breaths living formations
all around her

ii

Winter Fingerprints

I was praying with my hands
on your hips.

And that was how I knew
the body's

limitations.
Come January the snow

would make its bank
against our torsos,

and ice would be
the pause

between heartbeats, between breaths.
I would whisper

into the curve of an earlobe
while the sky

ashed around us,
forming gray flowers.

What shall we do
in this life

with a scaffolding of bones
beneath our skin?

You touched my face
with breath.

This was languaging
without spittle

or tongue,
the teeth not yet

breaking the surface
of the apple.

Anthem (Snow)

When we first moved in together, there was somewhere
a dull blade of moon and expansive fields like inland seas.

And surely the clouds were visible to many, a distant carapace
of sky, and snow tapered along fences into sharpness.

And what of the honking horns in cities and bus doors
whooshing open then closed? And lovers gazing at ceilings

and whispering words familiar in the throat, ones mouthed
so many times before, some great cacophonous voice?

Love, then, was the salt breeze and the tufts of weeds
growing in sand and taillights on the freeway after dark

and a crack in the pale blue of a robin's egg held in a palm.
The attenuated hours became the raft on which we rode,

the sea beneath us black or gray or green or blue with love,
and somewhere, always, the propeller in the chest quickened

or shut down, some circuitry of brain illuminating its own
existence. And I remember the heft of your suitcase

in my hand. You were climbing from your car,
and everywhere a chaos of snow fell around us.

father beats his sons
beneath an unmoored moon

& the ground is wet from the day's rain & the boys

are a covenant   & the boys listen for signs in hoot owl calls

& the brothers accept that the moon is an offering & their father

is a bear that emerged from his drunken den   & the sky says

here is the hole in my body from where the days crawl

& the earth says *here is the place from where everyone is born*

& the vultures say *tomorrow we will suture the sky to make it fast*

& the boys dream that night that they can see through bones of the earth

dream that the night sky is plucked out like an eye   that their father

is a garment of clouds or a gathering of crows come morning

so many dark beaks   & the brothers petition the earth

to make of the days something fetid & true   & the brothers lie awake

& tell themselves that absence is a country & pain another place

on the road of the years & they can lash the bones of that country

into a raft   & ride it across the eyehole of the sky

yellowjacket dreams

the boys see them building a nest in the backyard
flying in and out of an opening of dirt
some fissure in the fabric of everything
& in the dense heat of noon the yellowjackets swarm
into a strange vortex   as ancient
as the cuneiform writing of deer prints the boys
see sometimes in the soft mud beside the creek
& in their dreams the boys stand amid
the levitating wasps with their eyes closed
& arms spread   & the creatures land one by one
on their skin   & sting them on their necks & hands
& faces & backs   & then the boys murder
the yellowjackets one by one   swatting
& stomping them with their shoes   & then the boys
crawl into that opening of dirt & listen
for the frenetic hum of their own bodies

Anthem

I believed, then, that the lovers were the dark waters

of the river, the skin of moonlight

staining the summer leaves. And always

there was the loneliness of floating, the clouds

on their conveyor belts, the ridge of mountain

disembodied beyond the raised road. It seemed

there was something metaphysical in the salt of the skin,

in arms and legs that longed to be a ship or a raft.

In one dream the river opened, finally, into black sea,

and the lovers began swimming out toward

the lip of the world. Each arm stroke

splashed into prayer. Each kick was a new world.

And the stars drifted perched upon the waves.

Primitive Prayers

Nothing is more present
than memory, the black flies

elevating their bodies
in the swales, the hours

dense with childhood, an estuary
of evening light becoming

a slow feast of years, the clouds
with their migrations, a V of geese

pressing a sharp prow into a cloud,
trees mute beyond the yard, a light

rain stammering. Death seeps into
the muscle and bone, we know,

secreting a cold moistness into
air, the smell of apples decaying

in the orchard. And the gums
of our riverbank twist with

living roots near where lovers,
after dark, climb from cars or trucks

and carry blankets along the distant
line of the fence. Each year,

it seems, is a blade of grass—
servile grass, profligate grass,

primitive grass. And snow arrives
come winter as though from

the portal of a dream, the dark sky
like the manic blown pupil

of an eye, the atavistic river
accepting cold into its depths.

Then wind cuts across the hardened
earth near the garden, making

sacred music, and the geese honk
otherworldly going past,

each new hour slipping forever
into its envelope of earth.

the midwest hangs itself while listening to bobolinks

& the birds know how to slow a lifetime's hands

how grass is not a quickness but a history

& once the midwest dreamed an epistle of moonlight

above the quiet houses   & once the midwest made a religion

out of the cadences of loam   though the skeletal remains

of the factories still wait amid the broken glass   still hold

themselves aloof in that same forgetful abeyance   & the midwest

studies how the stars after dark are open wounds   how legs

thrash before the toes point down   but here   now

there is something holy in a bobolink   holy in the spiral

staircase of dusk leading up & up to nowhere   in the clawgrip

of the clouds   & the sudden drop like a souvenir

Prayer Book

In Turner's *Fishermen at Sea*, clouds and water

are made of the same dumb substance,
though still a ghostly light

drifts into the center, this rough garment
the body knows to wear, the vow we make

to pare things down, to chisel years—
until to feel at all now is a pleasure, a bird

singing in someone else's garden.

the brothers try to drown each other
at guthrie quarry

for the water here is a green corridor   & the view from the top

is the first prophecy   & stones fly through the air & whistle

past their heads   & the myopia of summer reminds the boys

that death is yet another numerology   this counting while holding

a brother's head beneath the surface   & death is the squirming of arms

& legs to reach a first inheritance   some original body like a vigil

& the water says to the boys *i will marry you in stillness*

& the boys say to the water *we used to believe we were bound to the earth*

& sunlight dreams a darkness pooling around the lungs   dreams

a contagion in the nostrils & throat   & the brothers see giving in

as the only actual death   even later as they ride their bikes back

to their father's house   & keep trying to bump each other into traffic

City by the Sea

And so the hours passed like slow hooves.

And we watched the sky go gray
above the rooftops.

Then someone said it was going to snow,

but the breath of clouds remained
the same, each day slipping away
into the sea.

Waiting, then, was the tight space
beneath the ribcage, the soft voice
of wind in an alley.

And the sky above the buildings knew nothing
of our lives, and the water, in the distance,
seemed somehow incorporeal,

and then in darkness like the blown pupil of an eye.

We were learning, it seemed, to imagine snow falling
as though into an open grave. To imagine children
on the sidewalks reaching up

with exposed palms. *Let us pray*, the decades said
as we lay in bed at night
and dreamed of that confetti-white erasure,

of elegiac snow, gauzy snow, shy snow.

The Marriage We Carried in Our Pockets

Or sometimes watched drifting with the leaves,
some last confetti of yellow or brown. Or it existed

the way the juncos huddled beneath the thistle
feeder in winter, the way clouds spilled water

in May to soak the ground. Once we found it
in the attic in a steamer trunk, and another time

we closed it in a suitcase and drove it across
the countryside. And often we imagined that

the years were a locked door against which
we kept knocking to be admitted. And on the dresser

of the new house, I spilled the change of the marriage
into a heap, and later we sat on the back porch and watched

the nuptial clouds on their conveyor belts. And we slept
at night with the breaths of the marriage around us.

black cloth of sky (seen through
a pabst blue ribbon bottle)

father dreams drunk   dreams lucent hours of lying on his back
dreams of hollow logs of decades to crawl inside   & he speaks

with a clot of tongue   & he converses with his own thoughts
& he argues with every chimney smoke of memory   then sometimes

he leans in the doorway of the boys' bedroom   or he leans
in the doorway of his daughter's room   & he thinks

here is the slow mire   here is the incorporeal past   & once he drove
as a young man down from ohio to mississippi   & he gazed

at the flatness of the gulf   & he thought *if i walked out
on the plains of these waters i would sink   if i dipped my head*

beneath the waves i would swallow salt   & once in his 20s he stabbed
a man who punched him   & the man became another inescapable map

some geography of fury   & father dreams anger   dreams a red wraith
of sky   dreams blood horizons   & he skips years likes stones

across each imaginary ocean   & he lies beside his wife at night
& listens to the ships of her breaths   & those ships say

this is my leakage & these are my sails   & those ships say *we carry the years
like a withering*   then father drinks on the back porch   drinks

in his pickup   drinks at the kitchen table   drinks beneath the stars
& the stars say *this we know . . . the visible & the invisible are at war*

Dialogue and Asymmetry

The moon tonight is falling
into the chimney of the neighbor's house

in the way we believe we speak
to the years behind us,

whisper to them of the miraculous passage
of the hours. And if the moon knows

to whisper back, it is in the language
of stone walls and the scaffolding

of bones inside our bodies, this hinge
that never opens but is forever at the ready.

And the moon, tonight, seems to be
leaning its shoulder into the neighbor's roof,

and the house seems to be leaning its shoulder
into the darkness of the sky,

and I am thinking of how we slept so often
those first years with our legs and arms entwined.

Your hair, then, was a black veil spreading its ink
around us, some calligraphy like a sentence

sprawling and sprawling over decades,
becoming languorous with meaning.

And if the moon out the window
is the shape of a wheel ghosting some dark prairie,

what shape are we leaning
against a windowsill?

moon sonnet

the boys throw stones at the moon inside their dreams
& slit the moon's throat   drag the carcass to the earth and drown it
in the river   & the moon says *let me hold you in my arms*
& the boys say *you will bleed dark blood from your underbelly*
& the boys imagine smashing a stone to the moon's skull
& the moon says *i was hung by the neck in the sky*   & the boys
want to pluck out the moon's lone eye   want to bury the moon
in the sky's loam   & the moon reaches down with its soft hands
& the moon says *hush hush*   & the brothers dream that they carry
the moon in their pockets   drop it from the quarry   hear it splash
into the black   & the boys say to the moon *please come down*
& stay with us   & the moon says to the boys *this is my body*
& the boys roll over in their sleep   & the boys are restless
in their dreams   & the boys long to burn the moon to ash

Tethered

The years, then, like the smell of damp grass.

The night sky forever far away beyond the ridge
where a train is praising the valley
and the tupelos are blooming
or shedding their obovate leaves.

Now it is beginning, soon it is beginning.

The days in human shape, loam and leaves
and tar-colored bark. Signs like a strange
burning wheel, a path in the woods growing
slowly more wild then disappearing.

The hours tethered to earth the way the moon
is tethered to the sky.

How grief endures. The field taking its deposition
of the river. You hear a certain timbre in your voice,
a hesitation, like something unsettled—

leaves drifting and sinking
in brackish water.

Each small and incidental moment
existing soundlessly as in a dream.

father gets drunk with the moon

& once the boys find their father passed out in the back bed

of the truck   & find the moon passed out on the surface

of the pond   & the moon & the father sing in sepulchral voices

skin-damp as a tongue   & sing of the years being stripped down

& once the boys find the moon passed out at the bottom of the stairs

find their father passed out on a shelf of the treetops   & their father instructs

the moonlight in ways to suffocate the land   & the moonlight instructs

the father in ways to drown in the black waters   & once the boys

find their father passed out in the field beyond the barn

& the snow makes of his body an occultation   & it makes of his body

something the boys approach cautiously to poke with a stick

feral trains

grandmother dreams of a pupil of light   something

small enough to prophesize loss   dreams of pockmarks

on the surface of a pond in a faint rain   & since her body

is alluvial   & since her body is a gathering

she imagines that the long throat of the decades sings

in plosives of forgetfulness   as though waking in a dark room

at night is a slow dance   & the trains in the distance

seem loosed upon the earth with their ghostly blossomings

& grandmother imagines sitting with her grandchildren on an imaginary

back porch & watching each moon floating amid the dark

congealing river   & she remembers once dreaming

that a moon-flower pulsed atop the watery grave

& when she plucked it from the sky & held it close

to her body   it pressed itself against her chest to suckle

History of the Wheel

When we first met, the fish-bone clouds
settled in above our lives.

And the curves of the body became, at night,
another dark hillside,

the ghostly hands of the animal within,
as primitive as weeds, which sway

the way a shoulder dips.
Even darkness breathes. Even light

bends across a horizon.
We held each other in a claustrophobia

of motion, this wheel that turns and turns
on the smallness of an axis.

Ghost Fire

And often, still, we are unsure. Something twists up and up to become a stair. And what is the end for? Who would stop here and dream such accumulations? Once there was a fire. It was sinew and bone. It was a small thing. They thought their ribs curved into it, that the scaffolding within them flared up into a ghost. And they are trying to dream the smoke of it. The real is always at the mercy of the mud of the river. Their lines cast out and out. Their bobbers float. Or if they hear a breath of a syllable, it means the crows have come to find them. Don't move. Don't draw in air. This is what the world says. And the moon at night grows bloated then decays. And the stars are carrion flies. And they search the ashes for bits of bone.

renunciation

mother is who is on the other side
mother is dim evening light and the bent neck of cattails

mother kneels by her tomato plants
& if her boys see her from the house

it is the kind of sight that cannot hold the story in its hands
& if she speaks it is the breeze rustling leaves in someone else's yard

yet father is the murky water of the river
& father is the clouds giving birth at night to loud rain

& father is the pounding of footsteps in the hall
& the blood light come morning wounding the slit of sky

but mother is the catfish that does not thrash
or even heave when it is dragged from the river

& mother is the slow mire & the space between heartbeats
& the nearly-invisible gnats resurrected come summer in the weeds

& mother's boys almost spy her out the window
& mother's boys imagine that the heat of summer is a crucifixion

that the tomatoes are dead hearts or green hearts
& the hours are calcified to bone

are prefigured as moonlight
& mother lies in bed at night & dreams of drizzle

warm as spit
dreams of open eyes of fields

then rises in the night to stand on the back porch
& touch her hand to shadows

   to be anointed by shadows
& to study the way the fireflies

   keep changing their minds
about existence

there is inside the brothers a trajectory

of letting go   something hardening into flung stone

some hollowing at the center of their bones   or maybe

the years are shriveled creatures   & the boys are the entrails

of the bullfrog they saw once squashed flat on the raised road

& the brothers studied the dead grass at that road's edge

& that dead grass studied the boys leaning down   & once

they hanged the neighbor's cat & buried it   & the cat

said *here is my alluvium*   & the boys said *the years*

are a lunar tug   & they spoke some nights

of how the stars invented themselves as gritty sand

& how all longing was epileptic   some inward thrashing

but mostly they aimed themselves out in one direction

& that direction said *every night is a black tongue*

& the boys said *this is my nocturne*   then morning slit

the night's throat & made it bleed

Mud Words

I think there is something to postmortem words

between lovers. An asylum of coffee cups is arranged

on the table. There should be ablutions when the sexual

theater ends. This is our ritual of the conspicuous pungency

of loss. We loved, we tell ourselves, with a temperate

constancy of sorrow. We wanted with a small euphoria

of disappointment. We planted our needs like a bulb

in the depths of the earth, and what emerged

was proportional, small as a breath,

deceptive as the pedestrian aphorism.

the brothers' one true home is in their bodies

though once they lived inside their mother   who lived inside her husband's hous
who lived inside the crows of his own thoughts   though sister was born first

& sister rode her stick horse in the drive   & sister counted *one two three*
when her parents fought   as though each breath were a kind of numerology

& in her dreams mother imagined her boys crawling again from the mud of her bo
carrying on their skin an augury of blood   & the boys became like the bats

in the backyard zigzagging through the air   became like the death flies
hovering above the roadkill beside the mailbox   & the brothers said to the flies

this is the measure of a life   & the flies said to the roadkill *this is*
the great mystery   & the roadkill said to the sky *here is the world*

stripped down to nothing   & the boys poked the roadkill with a stick
& the stick said *if you were a door i would step through it*

Five Omens in Nine Days

Always there were signs: geese
with their otherworldly Vs,

juncos pecking thistle from
the ice, the skinned days

half-buried in the shadows
And once we spotted

a lone hearse of a cloud
amid an interrogation of light

along the ridge. And we
held each other like tufts

of fur clinging to a wire
fence, like a scattering

of feathers. And the sky,
that winter, had its cobalt hat,

and bone shards of moon
poked through the clouds

after dark. And everywhere
the funerary snow came down.

the old men climb a flight of stairs to go to bed

& so they step up & up   their legs stiffening into ancient stones

the years veiled over & pleated   their hair like ghost heads

of dandelions   & as they rise they imagine the ascent

as one more sagging death march   mute as the splinters

on the wooden railings   & when they reach their beds

they dream that the world outside the house is a kind

of fallen harmony   & maybe their wives lie beside them

like dropped petals   & maybe there is a thorn in the skin

of the night sky beyond the windows   something hooked & howling

& come morning they stand at the top of the stairs & imagine

that each step downward is like waiting for fruit to fall

drowned boy

or now such occultations   eddies   swirls

night twitching beneath stars   some ribbon

of darkness snaking out   bright afterthoughts of light

across a current   & the river says *here are my ancient signs*

then morning brings another gray foot of day   & morning brings

all certainty of loam   & the boy's mother calls across the lowlands

her breaths dissolving into mist   the audible truth

of it reeling in the shallows   songs like fissures

of air   contagion light amid the trees   & still she walks

some mire of dream as translucent as fish eggs   birds stilled

above her on the limbs   hours pulsing while clouds

impale the sky   & the river says *the sun transforms*

its shape into a claw   & the river says *here is*

my shoulder like a lullaby

this town is roadkill fed on by crows

the roads here are straight as the end of days
& night skies are black as pitch
                                    so let us pray

to the bobby pins that let loose the hair
of decades   to the same sleepy fields

with their same folded wings   & to the quarry
forever opening its animal eye
                                    & to the corn growing

so high it strains the neck to look up
                                    & up

& say there is church, church, bar, bar, bar
& bar, church, bar, bar, bar

then a tourniquet of hours that dream another tightening
in the chest   another funeral tie around each neck

& the preacher on sunday placing bandages
on his savior's seeping wrists
                                    while the pews

are forever a wooden boat rocked in a storm
& afterwards everyone steps
                                    into the light

& squints across the road
to the high school football field

with its blessings
                    of trampled grass

Grass Prayers

And if she loves the calling jays,
the carnal heat of late July, my wife imagines

wading with me into decades:
work then children then illnesses then dying.

In the dream the lake beyond the field
is the bright iris of an eye, the stigmata

leaf shadows staining earth. And though
she knows that prayers are older

than the prophet grass, she imagines
speaking to the half-blind garden wall

with its crumbling stones, speaking
to the primitive voices of crows.

Each new word arches its back in grass,
this dumb substance we carry in the mud

of our bodies, how the preacher moon
drifts desiccated in a night sky.

signs

after their father dies they see his boots
overturned by the barn   deer prints

in the shape of his eyes   a mummery
of clouds   & the grass in winter

becomes a tabletop of snow   & the boys hold
their breaths & think   *death is a moon*

with a stationary dance   & they listen
to an emission of crow calls from the fields

the days thrashing like catfish dragged
to the bank   & they dream their father

buried hard as a bulb in the earth   stiff
as his clothes still waiting in his closet

the weeks fragile as discarded snakeskins
& the boys imagine death as a weigh station

or a hawk hanging crucified in air   & the boys
think   *last fall the trees coughed & the acorns*

dropped into the yard   & the boys think   *death*
is a train in the distance   one you hear but cannot see

& their father whispers in their thoughts
i wish i could bring you here to join me

The Old Worlds

Vultures offer their requiem at first light.
They live by memory, by rote.

Something dies or lives.
And a simulacrum of my breath this morning

is a cloud. I walk to be away.
Original humans whispered

their passwords to the liminal, spoke to moon
souls, to oracles of bones.

I see a raccoon belly up with the primitive
music of raw innards. The grass

is yellow-brown beside my fence.
The old world tells a story to the beautiful

wings of retreating carrion birds,
instructions written into the eye and mind.

The world must be coming to an end. The world
must know this constitutes desire.

blind the years

what we can't see is everywhere   blotting-paper sky
years with beautiful shoulders   children playing

jump rope beneath windows   broken vessels of memory
so many limericks of rote life   walking through

nameless markers   knowing we are buried somewhere
eyes shut against the field's edge   yet we say what matters

is the method   this given name for whatever place
exists inside our bodies   vowels released like balloons

into the evening air   god the skinny stalk wavering in the wind
nobody here except the myth of it   one more way of making the soil

parallel to our hands   the mother trees outstretching every arm
& all of us flinging bits of breath to make a map   or now

the infinite in the evening's yawn   our eyes clicking shut
like a doll's   the way we keep turning to see what's behind us

the brothers fall in love

with horseflies & the broken vessel of the days & the skull of moon
& the bloodletting clouds & the broken eye sockets of dreams &
the fevered death rattles of snores levitating from their father's room
& the starving dog & the knife that slices off the squirrel's tail &
the confetti of feathers as the pellet strikes & the smell of their boy
flesh & the bloodied meat & the potions of fetid night rain & the
neighbor girl they spy through her bathroom window & the crude
words they write in chalk on her driveway & the bats at twilight that
appear like broken chips of sky & the rotting loam inside their chests
& the neighbor girl they call names on the school bus & the cemetery
crows that float above the graves & the raccoon at the roadside with
its heavy bloat & the neighbor girl who retreats inside her house
when they ride by on their bikes & the dead bones of trees that stand
up by the river & the sacred object of the girl's notebook they steal
from her at school then adorn with drawings of penises & boobs &
the boot that crushes the head of a snake & the snapping turtle they
crack open at the river & the girl who gives them the sacrament of
the finger the evenings they chase her into her yard

In the Kingdom

And so, in the sixth month,
we lost the child.

And our exiled breaths
slipped from the sleeve of the earth.

Some mornings there was a small ache
of mud in the garden.

And once the skin of sky opened in winter
and let down white ash,

the morphine clouds drifting past
above our heads. We could imagine

dirt sleeping in the fields, imagine
the primal indifference of weeds.

And I thought, those first years,
that the rivulets of rain on the driveway

were an ancient voice.
And I watched the stars

dissolving at dawn above the ridge, light
merging into a single line, a red smear evolving

or devolving. And what remained, later,
was snow drifting against the fence,

the anonymous juncos at the feeder.
Decades became a bolt

on a door—sometimes latched, sometimes open.
And light passed without fanfare through

the windows into rooms
where we were living. We imagined

the years dividing themselves into an empty
vase on a table and water running

from a faucet. And then, after a life of this,
we found in the manifold rooms of old age

that one bedroom with its east-facing
windows. There were omens

of what would not leave us be: a cautionary
fire in the distance, a wilderness of birdcalls

at dusk. And when we spoke, we imagined
that the moon was a severed tongue.

iv

ontological snow

nearly every morning   it's not so easy   to be proportional

or a certain shape of being   not while a diagram of wind

is whistling through the window jamb

or i wake to the same vague   thought   that everything

is either subliminal or an echo   & the conviction feels

in this half-absent state   like a vaporous anchor that used to hold

the clouds in place before it fell away   or maybe i rise and see

out the window that it snowed in the night   & the democracy

of white is not quite a subtraction or an addition   but more

a pale fixity   of whatever exists without boundaries

so isn't actually real   & somehow this sense summons

its own intensifications   of unknowing   the birdfeeder

with its little white cap   the snowdrifts whispering against

the fence   & of course there is the blurring of feeling

in the shower   the blindfolded sensations   that seem

like a face gazing up plaintively   through a membrane or barrier

or maybe   on the way to work   i see that an incision in a cloud

is letting through one single cartoon cliché   of a revelation that seems a kind of disembarking   new day beneath

a gray morgue   of winter sky

white sky

these robes of morning
make a fence of the world

some sedge of sky as the rain stops
something found

& then abandoned   i used to believe
that the years were made

of grass & shadows
& dense summer heat

something stewing in its own juices
some loam of hours

thickened with prophecy
there was the summer my brother

and i slept some nights in hammocks
on our father's back porch   slept

while the mosquitoes
anointed us in blood

then were awakened mornings
by an intruder sun

& the broken vessels
of the trees behind the house

how whisperless the sky
seemed   how emptied of its own being

as we rose in our bodies
to step into it

the moon opens & closes its gate

& the lateness of the hour is a thin gauze   & the moon a dead horse

above the river   & the boys' dead father is chimney smoke passing

over the slanted roofs   & the roofs are stooped shoulders

& at the funeral the scalpels of wind tear across the land

& the boys that night feel a twitch in their knees as they sleep

a loose fold of a dream flapping its hinge   & they conjure

a kind of breath that knows to huddle quietly in doorways

that whistles faintly like the distant flares of cigarettes

& the boys pretend that their father is that crow that oars out

above the fields   black sails above the snow's belly

& they dream of dark tongues   of the way-stations of the dead

some beautiful murky language beneath the shaved skull of moon

& when they wake they study the ponderous slowness of the river

Grass Alchemy

I am dreaming, today, of the mutable shapes

of years, how a thin strip of fertile soil covers clay.

I see the bluing light of summer, see the cracked

vessel of drifting clouds. Or say I view our lives the way

a pulse throbs in the ears, or imagine sap waiting

in a winter tree but never freezing. And through

the western windows I watch the flames of yellow grass

while listening to the voices of the days. Sometimes birds

call without meaning we can understand. And soon

we collect the decades—water settling into brine.

I study morning fog as though it is a silent

drum. I know that breath itself is a kind of marching,

that each new year is a limp body dragged from the coldness

of the water, is the air I force down into waiting lungs.

Earthly Displays

I step out the back door and put on the mantle
of the world, stand in grass beneath the fat

hats of clouds—not the holy rollers who speak
in tongues but the shaved skull of the early

hour, broken only by a covenant of crows
at the field's edge, where first dawn is slowly

smudging into view. You tell me how your mother
left small flowers of red on cigarette butts in bar ashtrays.

Gray smoke drifted always above her head. Here is
the language of grief, acorns falling into the small

garden pond beside us, landing with a weighty
splash, otherworldly—some preacher saying

Jesus on Sundays, the name like a fat bulb
pressed into the mud of the earth.

the art of divination

mother is the snakeskin that disintegrates   is the moldering log
     whispering from the woods

& so the years pass   & the loose earth collects in the windowsills
     & mother feels the salt

sweat on her skin   how it cleaves & forgets   & when her sons are born
     she conjures them

from leaf meal and dust   & dreams that the moon suckles at her chest
     with its hard skull

of bone   & she imagines that all life is a fermentation   is the apples
     in summer decaying

on the ground into vinegar   worried by wasps   & she studies the
     way her husband

comports his adam's apple in his throat   twitches it even in his sleep
     this living

creature that is stuck there and aching to get loose   & her boys swim
     in the brackish

river   & she conducts her necromancy with a dead crow at the roadside
     how its wings

flutter each time a car whooshes by   & when her boys are young
     their cries split

the night   as disturbing as ammonia in the air   burning her nostrils
     & their hard skulls

bruise her chest   & their gums bite down   & she closes her eyes into it

Chicago

Today an outstretched arm
came toward me

just before the Clark Street Bridge,
and the teenager pressed

the sharp point of the barrel
into the folds of my ribs,

and I was thinking, in that moment,
of describing snow as "white ash"

or "mummified,"
though didn't that call to mind

The Mummy's Hand or *The Mummy's Shroud?*
And then the boy asked

in such a breathy voice for my wallet
and watch that it seemed

the words were snow.

Old Mud

It isn't simply the mother tongue of leaves rustling in the woods,

the black sky above the river with its fissures of stars.

It is the erasure of storm clouds lumbering from the west,

the ghost dance of the back gate banging the post. And here

is the fallen log hollow at its center, this opening where I burrow in,

the smells of loam inside a neurasthenic dream. I come here

to hold my breath, to feel the cold reach forth with a dispatch of lips.

And in the dream the bodies of animals decay around me.

I hear the silence of them brooding, know the mud of them,

and the austerity and the gentleness of holding still.

sister rides her stick horse toward eternity

here is my back to carry you the driveway says
& sister says *ride ride*   & sister says *we will ride*
into the sea & swim   & in her mind the horse

is a raft   & in her mind her dead father
is the sea   & the sea says *i am the eye of the sky*
& sister rides the stick horse to the mailbox

then back   & the mailbox says *your hooves*
are tall ladders   & mother watches out the window
& mother thinks *my daughter is a storm surge*

my daughter is an orbit   & the stick horse says
the glassy sky is a country   & the grass beside
the driveway says *i am the earth's fingertips*

& the girl clomps the same foot forward again & again
& the horse is a bird burrowing into clouds
& the horse says *all motion is a ghost*

History

I know my breaths are out there in the world.

This happens the way love does. There is so little

to see of the miles. And later, at home, I peer

out a window at my own reflection gazing back.

In the allegory of the cave, the shadows on the wall

become insect splatters on a windshield when I drive.

And so I keep trying to decide if the remains of a sliver

of a fly's wing is an omen. Some say love is

a hundred tongues, but when I count I think of litter bearers

straining. I confess to not knowing where words go.

One moment they are here, but then they are wind

or snow coming down. I name each breath

for centuries, each whisper for another road

on which we hurry down with vanishing.

the geography where the boys live includes an unlatched gate

because sometimes the dead oak
               wonders

what hammering of sound encases
                morning

like thrown stones
          some mummification

of sleeping
        deranging

boy breath & boy sweat
           & soon they run

out the back door
        woodbound

smashing garter snake heads
            toads

boys loosed into the lowlands
            conjuring

that old gnaw
        primitive as spit

sepulchral rain
        pockmarking the river

brothers like formaldehyde
           clouds

brothers like bruised
        fruit

dreaming of squirrels
                    blood-red

& oozing
            every occultation

of fever until mother
                    calls

& the house around them
                            hardens

then ferments
            as the boys sit

at the supper table
                    then later sleep

& dream
            while the gate

opens & closes
                its animal eye

Wind Metaphysics

The sky has forgotten we have mouths,

words to oar like rowboats

in a lake. And if there is a God, he closes

the blinds so he can sleep. I dream sometimes

I am riding in a glass-bottomed boat

and see, below, the lives of the dead, as serene

as scar tissue, as familiar as winter air

seeping through a window jamb.

Divining the Mountain

For years I have studied the ebbtide of evening
drifting along the distant ridge. Little changes

on the mountain except the spells of rain
and sun and mist and snow. And it seems possible

to dream the slow pirouette of seasons, the sacred
freight of years. One summer a neighbor girl

was struck by a school bus along the mountain's base
and died. And two springs later my wife had her

miscarriage, the cortex of stars appearing like so many
bees humming above the mountain's hive. The road

beyond our house is often overrun with weeds, and we
see the teenagers come summer lying on their blankets

by the river. The sky beyond the mountain plants
the bulbs of longing deep, and the clouds at dusk

appear like bits of burning leaves shriveling at their edges.
And after the rains each year, the sky is a secret room.

We come from alluvium, I believe, and listen
to the canopy of trees conversing with the wind.

Let us be carried now, I sometimes think.
Let the cadence-moon lie down. And my wife and I walk

sometimes along the bottom of the mountain.
It seems there are holes in the hours, what slips

through. And if it is night, we speak of the wafer-thin
starlight on the ridge. And we recall the leech that once

affixed itself to the soft of my wife's ankle when we
waded in the river. And the blood of dawn when

we walk in early light is always rapture. And one
morning we come across a cluster of trillium

not far from the river's bank, the white mouths
open as though to swallow ghosts.

Winter Trance

I have been studying the migration
of the years, the dull heat of their passage

a strange fire. And because they are holy,
gravity slips through them, these cycles

of sleeping and waking as quiet
as the space between heartbeats,

the stillness of January fields,
the men by the fence at the roadside

in their orange jumpsuits,
the winter crows oaring out of the trees.

About the Author

Doug Ramspeck is the author of eight previous collections of poetry, one collection of short stories, and a novella. His most recent book, *Book of Years* (2021), is published by Cloudbank Books. Individual poems have appeared in *The Southern Review, The Georgia Review, Slate, Missouri Review,* and many other literary journals. His story "Balloon" was listed as a Distinguished Story for 2018 in *The Best American Short Stories.* A retired professor from The Ohio State University, he lives in Black Mountain, North Carolina. His author website can be found at dougramspeck.com.

About The Word Works

Since its founding in 1974, The Word Works has steadily published volumes of contemporary poetry and presented public programs. Its imprints include The Washington Prize, The Tenth Gate Prize, The Hilary Tham Capital Collection, and International Editions.

Monthly, The Word Works offers free programs in its Café Muse Literary Salon. Starting in 2023, the winners of the Jacklyn Potter Young Poets Competition will be presented in the June Café Muse program.

As a 501(c)3 organization, The Word Works has received awards from the National Endowment for the Arts, the National Endowment for the Humanities, the D.C. Commission on the Arts & Humanities, the Witter Bynner Foundation, Poets & Writers, The Writer's Center, Bell Atlantic, the David G. Taft Foundation, and others, including many generous private patrons.

An archive of artistic and administrative materials in the Washington Writing Archive is housed in the George Washington University Gelman Library. The Word Works is a member of the Community of Literary Magazines and Presses and its books are distributed by Small Press Distribution.

wordworksbooks.org

About the Tenth Gate Prize

The Tenth Gate Prize honors mid-career poets writing in English. Entry is open to authors of at least two previously published full-length poetry collections (excluding chapbooks, self-published volumes, and forthcoming titles). A prize of $1000 and publication of the full-length collection is awarded annually. Kasey Jueds serves as Series Editor; the winning manuscript is selected by an outside judge. The submission period is June 1 through July 15.

Leslie McGrath founded the series in 2014 to honor Jane Hirshfield's essay collection *Nine Gates: Entering the Mind of Poetry* and each winner's sustained dedication to developing a unique poetics.

PAST WINNERS:

Jennifer Barber, *Works on Paper*, 2015
Carolyn Guinzio, *A Vertigo Book*, 2020
Christine Hamm, *Gorilla*, 2019
Lisa Lewis, *Taxonomy of the Missing*, 2017
Brad Richard, *Parasite Kingdom*, 2018
Roger Sedarat, *Haji As Puppet*, 2016
Lisa Sewell, *Impossible Object*, 2014

CPSIA information can be obtained
at www.ICGtesting.com
Printed in the USA
LVHW051125240323
PP17697400010B/11